TABLE OF CONTENTS

Workbook Answers

Chapter 1 - Whole Numbers

Pg 6

1.

1	5	6	3	2	7	8	2
Ten Millions	Millions	Hundred Thousands	Ten Thousands	Thousands	Hundreds	Tens	Ones

2.

2	4	8	7	9	3	6	0
Ten Millions	Millions	Hundred Thousands	Ten Thousands	Thousands	Hundreds	Tens	Ones

3.

6	2	1	5	8	5	2	4
Ten Millions	Millions	Hundred Thousands	Ten Thousands	Thousands	Hundreds	Tens	Ones

4.

3	0	6	7	1	2	3	4
Ten Millions	Millions	Hundred Thousands	Ten Thousands	Thousands	Hundreds	Tens	Ones

5.

5	2	1	9	7	3	0	5
Ten Millions	Millions	Hundred Thousands	Ten Thousands	Thousands	Hundreds	Tens	Ones

6.

8	3	4	9	8	1	4	7
Ten Millions	Millions	Hundred Thousands	Ten Thousands	Thousands	Hundreds	Tens	Ones

Pg 7

7	4	8	4	2	2	7	1	9
Hundred Millions	Ten Millions	Millions	Hundred Thousands	Ten Thousands	Thousands	Hundreds	Tens	Ones

1.

3	2	9	6	0	8	1	1	4
Hundred Millions	Ten Millions	Millions	Hundred Thousands	Ten Thousands	Thousands	Hundreds	Tens	Ones

2.

1	2	4	3	7	5	2	7	7
Hundred Millions	Ten Millions	Millions	Hundred Thousands	Ten Thousands	Thousands	Hundreds	Tens	Ones

3.

7	4	1	5	8	8	3	7	9
Hundred Millions	Ten Millions	Millions	Hundred Thousands	Ten Thousands	Thousands	Hundreds	Tens	Ones

4.

5	0	4	2	6	7	3	3	2
Hundred Millions	Ten Millions	Millions	Hundred Thousands	Ten Thousands	Thousands	Hundreds	Tens	Ones

5.

9	7	2	1	1	4	0	8	9
Hundred Millions	Ten Millions	Millions	Hundred Thousands	Ten Thousands	Thousands	Hundreds	Tens	Ones

6.

Pg 8		Pg 9		Pg 10	
No.	Answer	No.	Answer	No.	Answer
1	3,000	1	24,453	1	900 + 400 = 1,300
2	9,000	2	55,718	2	500 + 500 = 1,000
3	1,000	3	19,554	3	100 + 600 = 700
4	8,000	4	28,132	4	400 + 700 = 1,100
5	3,000	5	12,966	5	900 - 500 = 400
6	4,000	6	93,359	6	800 - 200 = 600
7	6,000	7	96,591	7	600 - 500 = 100
8	8,000	8	56,772	8	400 - 200 = 200
9	6,000	9	83,297		
10	2,000	10	27,915		
11	40,000	11	35,212		
12	20,000	12	62,689		
13	90,000	13	49,212		
14	60,000	14	79,359		
15	70,000	15	93,756		
16	80,000	16	41,328		
17	30,000	17	43,957		
18	40,000	18	14,161		
19	20,000	19	93,564		
20	50,000	20	39,817		
21	300,000				
22	600,000				
23	200,000				
24	500,000				
25	200,000				
26	300,000				
27	900,000				
28	600,000				
29	800,000				
30	100,000				

	Pg 11		Pg 12		Pg 13	
No.	**Answer**	**No.**	**Answer**	**No.**	**Answer**
1	6,000 + 4,000 = 10,000	1	1,225	1	6,515
2	5,000 + 1,000 = 6,000	2	1,024	2	12,834
3	9,000 + 7,000 = 16,000	3	1,580	3	12,670
4	5,000 + 5,000 = 10,000	4	742	4	11,229
5	3,000 + 6,000 = 9,000	5	1,261	5	16,342
6	8,000 + 7,000 = 15,000	6	1,111	6	8,877
7	2,000 + 5,000 = 7,000	7	1,353	7	5,300
8	4,000 + 5,000 = 9,000	8	1,632	8	11,866
9	9,000 + 500 = 9,500	9	1,236	9	13,940
10	4,000 - 2,000 = 2,000	10	1,430	10	9,715
11	9,000 - 5,000 = 4,000			11	15,009
12	7,000 - 6,000 = 1,000			12	5,461
13	5,000 - 3,000 = 2,000			13	4,177
14	9,000 - 8,000 = 1,000			14	15,408
15	4,000 - 2,000 = 2,000			15	13,512
16	4,000 - 800 = 3,200			16	24,745
17	6,000 - 2,000 = 4,000			17	10,693
18	8,000 - 6,000 = 2,000			18	14,319
				19	14,792
				20	14,112

Pg 14		Pg 15		Pg 16	
No.	Answer	No.	Answer	No.	Answer
1	23,795	1	104,654	1	596,052
2	16,340	2	188,944	2	977,698
3	16,891	3	144,072	3	1,160,308
4	23,486	4	189,476	4	1,097,102
5	18,748	5	104,323	5	1,089,063
6	22,475	6	103,894	6	1,283,759
7	20,531	7	156,084	7	1,336,765
8	13,385	8	140,874	8	845,509
9	13,938	9	184,913	9	1,051,175
10	19,146	10	147,781	10	1,085,891
11	17,264	11	57,012	11	1,975,054
12	17,039	12	183,425	12	841,668
13	16,951	13	131,969	13	1,410,112
14	14,558	14	101,039	14	1,518,639
15	22,189	15	184,161	15	2,240,839
16	14,766	16	115,576	16	720,411
17	21,953	17	83,250	17	1,776,777
18	13,765	18	68,871	18	1,577,184
19	8,331	19	174,540	19	1,304,447
20	18,795	20	264,261	20	1,662,926

Pg 17		Pg 18		Pg 19	
No.	Answer	No.	Answer	No.	Answer
1	12,052,629	1	443	1	1,112
2	7,888,122	2	452	2	1,111
3	17,265,467	3	143	3	3,781
4	21,709,039	4	284	4	2,779
5	14,622,984	5	539	5	1,756
6	11,129,457	6	118	6	6,487
7	19,771,741	7	861	7	7,511
8	17,143,156	8	451	8	2,264
9	10,170,485	9	252	9	524
10	14,603,355	10	129	10	5,685
11	23,268,932	11	291	11	327
12	13,589,274	12	450	12	2,047
13	15,296,451	13	288	13	4,635
14	17,280,455	14	457	14	2,059
15	12,562,642	15	432	15	5,475
16	15,576,391			16	2,889
17	15,540,467			17	1,454
18	15,214,301			18	916
19	22,688,631			19	2,755
20	20,429,648			20	2,747

Pg 20		Pg 21		Pg 22	
No.	Answer	No.	Answer	No.	Answer
1	2,786	1	131,482	1	592,288
2	25,038	2	507,851	2	1,409,294
3	21,376	3	277,758	3	5,730,630
4	36,508	4	34,013	4	2,437,389
5	20,756	5	778,375	5	2,113,834
6	16,804	6	191,436	6	5,220,339
7	20,507	7	411,246	7	7,314,169
8	4,557	8	352,113	8	2,876,907
9	37,509	9	221,963	9	3,135,552
10	38,809	10	232,179	10	5,127,660
11	18,499	11	47,078	11	1,801,944
12	26,055	12	181,244	12	4,683,052
13	15,864	13	426,781	13	3,125,607
14	43,464	14	151,044	14	4,587,627
15	45,132	15	374,747	15	3,670,658
16	46,172	16	96,861	16	3,371,113
17	18,489	17	189,668	17	6,478,871
18	21,529	18	412,017	18	2,359,169
19	57,435	19	199,681	19	3,467,162
20	76,939	20	619,306	20	2,282,335

Pg 23	
No.	Answer
1	13,138,506
2	30,680,207
3	22,547,298
4	35,657,655
5	7,593,206
6	46,473,155
7	55,559,777
8	89,277,747
9	34,798,707
10	19,262,091
11	86,135,587
12	29,474,647
13	64,926,012
14	43,864,964
15	30,236,771
16	37,778,627
17	81,291,709
18	37,006,688
19	56,327,553
20	38,185,370
21	66,798,298
22	75,126,679
23	15,285,265
24	32,454,367

Multiplication Table

X	1	2	3	4	5	6	7	8	9	10
1	1	2	3	4	5	6	7	8	9	10
2	2	4	6	8	10	12	14	16	18	20
3	3	6	9	12	15	18	21	24	27	30
4	4	8	12	16	20	24	28	32	36	40
5	5	10	15	20	25	30	35	40	45	50
6	6	12	18	24	30	36	42	48	54	60
7	7	14	21	28	35	42	49	56	63	70
8	8	16	24	32	40	48	56	64	72	80
9	9	18	27	36	45	54	63	72	81	90
10	10	20	30	40	50	60	70	80	90	100

X	4	5	6
6	24	30	36
5	20	25	30
4	16	20	24
3	12	15	18
2	8	10	12

1.

X	0	6	8	4	9
5	0	30	40	20	45
4	0	24	32	16	36
3	0	18	24	12	27

2.

X	2	3	4	5	6
10	20	30	40	50	60
11	22	33	44	55	66
12	24	36	48	60	72

3.

X	5	4	3
6	30	24	18
5	25	20	15
4	20	16	12
3	15	12	9
2	10	8	6

4.

Pg 28		Pg 29		Pg 30	
No.	Answer	No.	Answer	No.	Answer
1	260	1	1,968	1	735
2	147	2	3,168	2	1,536
3	108	3	432	3	1,944
4	552	4	1,944	4	3,216
5	456	5	2,088	5	5,525
6	392	6	1,036	6	3,404
7	116	7	935	7	3,354
8	160	8	2,046	8	1,015
9	476	9	1,656	9	3,196
10	747	10	288	10	1,800
				11	2,916
				12	5,568
				13	2,666
				14	8,740
				15	1,638
				16	7,200
				17	1,260
				18	6,566
				19	2,128
				20	3,705

Pg 31		Pg 32		Pg 33	
No.	Answer	No.	Answer	No.	Answer
1	42	1	7,383	1	25,532
2	640	2	4,921	2	28,896
3	57	3	22,016	3	36,096
4	72	4	16,524	4	11,713
		5	15,200	5	41,724
		6	24,999	6	40,807
		7	33,418	7	8,668
		8	5,640	8	15,876
		9	21,204	9	9,164
		10	53,952	10	31,178
		11	74,036	11	9,924
		12	37,905	12	18,278
		13	23,970	13	63,264
		14	50,007	14	45,689
		15	47,288	15	37,944
		16	45,045	16	22,743
		17	60,800	17	67,425
		18	57,072	18	14,314
		19	26,826	19	52,500
		20	83,040	20	63,624

Pg 34		Pg 35		Pg 36	
No.	Answer	No.	Answer	No.	Answer
1	3,381	1	77,532	1	31,572
2	956	2	102,915	2	68,740
3	1,536	3	167,684	3	152,875
4	608	4	253,425	4	32,147
		5	90,364	5	134,096
		6	376,467	6	174,801
		7	296,472	7	59,496
		8	230,278	8	226,023
		9	156,581	9	51,940
		10	254,910	10	128,808
		11	238,908	11	465,519
		12	404,247	12	382,932
		13	174,135	13	207,900
		14	606,268	14	641,056
		15	291,712	15	579,198
		16	260,559	16	269,244
		17	718,650	17	196,174
		18	524,688	18	793,945
		19	116,795	19	561,000
		20	488,166	20	885,024

Pg 37		Pg 38		Pg 39	
No.	Answer	No.	Answer	No.	Answer
1	157,680	1	66,794	1	418,284
2	222,221	2	69,689	2	250,355
3	79,530	3	258,937	3	584,168
4	269,346	4	128,853	4	826,428
5	63,784	5	230,955	5	1,660,480
6	120,825	6	130,104	6	1,604,106
7	568,874	7	180,048	7	785,436
8	182,400	8	103,170	8	588,707
9	145,148	9	350,966	9	1,668,172
10	616,710	10	247,648	10	1,940,352
11	110,670	11	140,140	11	3,672,774
12	106,524	12	101,106	12	1,145,224
13	308,355	13	203,109	13	555,182
14	445,060	14	285,950	14	3,315,922
15	473,324	15	104,328	15	3,198,804
		16	273,456	16	2,714,376
		17	180,560	17	4,070,924
		18	193,400	18	5,319,210
		19	87,269	19	5,624,400
		20	582,556	20	6,151,680

Pg 40		Pg 41	
No.	Answer	No.	Answer
1	2,133,216	1	6^4
2	345,555	2	3^3
3	1,143,539	3	5^3
4	1,110,444	4	7^4
5	2,901,440	5	9^5
6	2,880,279	6	8^6
7	1,093,680	7	2^6
8	855,218	8	4^4
9	1,770,131	9	5^3
10	1,327,798	10	6^5
11	4,844,560	11	7^7
12	1,395,384	12	2^3
13	3,455,694	13	3^4
14	630,343	14	9^6
15	1,953,252		
16	1,192,296		
17	5,038,836		
18	782,760		
19	8,052,375		
20	3,588,480		

Pg 42	
No.	Answer
1	9 x 9 x 9 = 729
2	5 x 5 x 5 x 5 x 5 = 3,125
3	8 x 8 x 8 x 8 = 4,096
4	2 x 2 x 2 x 2 x 2 x 2 x 2 x 2 x 2 = 512
5	6 x 6 x 6 x 6 = 1,296
6	4 x 4 x 4 x 4 x 4 = 1,024

Pg 43	
No.	**Answer**
1	$8 \times 8 = 64$
2	$6 \times 6 \times 6 \times 6 \times 6 = 7,776$
3	$7 \times 7 \times 7 \times 7 = 2,401$
4	$3 \times 3 \times 3 \times 3 \times 3 \times 3 \times 3 \times 3 = 6,561$
5	$4 \times 4 \times 4 = 64$
6	$5 \times 5 \times 5 \times 5 \times 5 = 3,125$

Pg 44	
No.	**Answer**
1	$9 < 16$
2	$64 > 9$
3	$16 < 25$
4	$7,776 > 64$
5	$27 > 25$
6	$125 > 49$
7	$4,096 > 125$
8	$216 < 729$
9	$256 < 4,096$
10	$25 < 81$
11	$343 > 4$
12	$256 > 9$
13	$512 > 16$
14	$81 < 729$
15	$36 < 49$

Chapter 3 – Division

No.	Pg 47 Answer	No.	Pg 48 Answer	No.	Pg 49 Answer	No.	Pg 50 Answer
1	16 r 1	1	13 r 2	1	8 trips	1	367 r 1
2	7 r 3	2	12 r 3	2	5 days	2	297 r 1
3	12 r 5	3	17 r 2	3	7 apples	3	134
4	45 r 1	4	10 r 2	4	9 cookies		
5	24 r 3	5	39				
6	14 r 2	6	11 r 3				
7	11 r 3	7	14 r 3				
8	33 r 1	8	21 r 1				
		9	15 r 1				
		10	41 r 1				
		11	10 r 7				
		12	12 r 5				

No.	Pg 51 Answer	No.	Pg 52 Answer	No.	Pg 53 Answer
1	153 r 2	1	65 r 7	1	1,241 r 2
2	32	2	68 r 4	2	569 r 5
3	196	3	129 r 4	3	1,522 r 1
4	139 r 2	4	338 r 1	4	630 r 1
5	90 r 5	5	21 r 2	5	1,325 r 3
6	148 r 4	6	250	6	2,178 r 3
7	188	7	104 r 1	7	632
8	148 r 1	8	122 r 6	8	968 r 1
9	207 r 1	9	37 r 4	9	450 r 4
10	232 r 2	10	275 r 2	10	1,867 r 1
11	111 r 1	11	113 r 1	11	1,142 r 2
12	140 r 6	12	368	12	999 r 3
13	423	13	84 r 12		
14	44 r 2	14	25		
15	204	15	87 r 1		
16	138	16	95 r 3		
17	192 r 2	17	453 r 1		
18	69 r 4	18	83 r 3		
19	75 r 6	19	97 r 2		
20	149 r 3	20	157		

No.	Pg 54 Answer	No.	Pg 55 Answer	No.	Pg 56 Answer
1	8,447 r 3	1	4540 r 3	1	52 Hours
2	21,624	2	15,337 r 3	2	13 Days
3	7,325 r 1	3	2,160 r 3	3	51 Hours
4	44,652 r 1	4	8,502 r 4	4	119 Sections
5	7,338 r 6	5	32,380 r 1		
6	18,027 r 4	6	10,381 r 4		
7	9,025	7	24,623 r 2		
8	18,327	8	10,136 r 7		
9	19,560 r 1	9	13,302		
10	4,050 r 6	10	8,324 r 3		
11	16,634 r 3	11	3,439 r 5		
12	7,800 r 7	12	14,152 r 4		

No.	Pg 57 Answer	No.	Pg 58 Answer	No.	Pg 59 Answer
1	21 r 8	1	22 r 5	1	207
2	19 r 10	2	24 r 18	2	148 r 6
3	20 r 9	3	20 r 9	3	137 r 40
4	37 r 5	4	5 r 4	4	111 r 27
5	15 r 24	5	43 r 1	5	226 r 12
6	13 r 24	6	22 r 7	6	259 r 11
7	16 r 16	7	22 r 4	7	213 r 14
8	12 r 9	8	22 r 9	8	291 r 3
9	10 r 53	9	21 r 20	9	203 r 30
10	19 r 19	10	17 r 8	10	118 r 3
		11	10 r 22	11	161 r 17
		12	10 r 26	12	205 r 10
		13	28 r 9		
		14	38 r 5		
		15	23 r 8		
		16	15 r 15		
		17	3		
		18	18 r 3		
		19	7 r 5		
		20	2 r 63		

Pg 60		Pg 61	
No.	Answer	No.	Answer
1	3,229 r 8	1	2,280 r 6
2	2,502 r 29	2	2,268 r 10
3	1,686 r 32	3	1,278 r 3
4	2,237 r 20	4	1,055 r 13
5	2,122 r 17	5	1,357 r 21
6	585 r 7	6	1,189 r 81
7	3,018 r 23	7	459 r 12
8	1,791 r 26	8	1,029 r 5
9	543 r 35	9	1,345 r 15
10	1,057 r 63	10	942 r 87
11	1,128 r 11	11	1,050 r 35
12	1,629 r 9	12	1,113 r 9

Pg 63		Pg 64	
No.	Answer	No.	Answer
1	$\dfrac{13}{15}$	1	$\dfrac{21}{73}$
2	$\dfrac{23}{37}$	2	$\dfrac{7}{28}$
3	$\dfrac{49}{80}$	3	$\dfrac{22}{89}$
4	$\dfrac{100}{109}$	4	$\dfrac{20}{146}$
5	$\dfrac{30}{64}$	5	$\dfrac{114}{634}$
6	$\dfrac{14}{21}$	6	$\dfrac{4}{12}$
7	$\dfrac{383}{865}$	7	$\dfrac{283}{759}$
8	$\dfrac{33}{55}$	8	$\dfrac{26}{56}$
9	$\dfrac{10}{13}$	9	$\dfrac{79}{207}$
10	$\dfrac{45}{74}$	10	$\dfrac{13}{49}$
11	$\dfrac{238}{250}$	11	$\dfrac{167}{277}$
12	$\dfrac{7}{94}$	12	$\dfrac{238}{534}$
		13	$\dfrac{66}{88}$
		14	$\dfrac{39}{129}$
		15	$\dfrac{189}{952}$

	Pg 65		
No.	**Answer**		
1	Tomatoes: $\frac{13}{28}$ Eggplants: $\frac{6}{28}$ Potatoes: $\frac{9}{28}$		
2	Blue Jays: $\frac{3}{15}$ Sparrows: $\frac{9}{15}$ Ducks: $\frac{6}{15}$ Eagles: $\frac{1}{15}$		
3	Bass: $\frac{2}{17}$ Trout: $\frac{6}{17}$ Guppies: $\frac{5}{17}$ Goldfish: $\frac{4}{17}$		
4	Hamburgers: $\frac{15}{76}$ Chicken Wings: $\frac{22}{76}$ Sausages: $\frac{39}{76}$		

Pg 66

$$\frac{1}{4}$$ $$=$$ $$\frac{2}{8}$$

$$\frac{2}{4}$$ $$=$$ $$\frac{4}{8}$$

$$\frac{3}{8}$$ $$=$$ $$\frac{6}{16}$$

$$\frac{5}{8}$$ $$=$$ $$\frac{10}{16}$$

Pg 67		Pg 68		Pg 69	
No.	Answer	No.	Answer	No.	Answer
1	$\frac{9}{9}, \frac{2}{3}$	1	$\frac{3}{5}, \frac{4}{5}$	1	$\frac{5}{7}+\frac{2}{7}=\frac{7}{7}$
2	$\frac{4}{4}, \frac{1}{3}$	2	$\frac{4}{6}, \frac{5}{6}$	2	$\frac{1}{5}+\frac{2}{5}=\frac{3}{5}$
3	$\frac{5}{5}, \frac{4}{7}$	3	$\frac{3}{7}, \frac{5}{7}$	3	$\frac{7}{10}+\frac{2}{10}=\frac{9}{10}$
4	$\frac{3}{3}, \frac{3}{8}$	4	$\frac{3}{8}, \frac{6}{8}$	4	$\frac{10}{12}+\frac{2}{12}=\frac{12}{12}$
5	$\frac{3}{3}, \frac{5}{7}$	5	$\frac{3}{5}, \frac{2}{5}$	5	$\frac{2}{9}+\frac{3}{9}=\frac{5}{9}$
6	$\frac{8}{8}, \frac{2}{5}$	6	$\frac{3}{4}, \frac{2}{4}$	6	$\frac{5}{7}+\frac{2}{7}=\frac{7}{7}$
7	$\frac{5}{5}, \frac{2}{5}$	7	$\frac{5}{7}, \frac{2}{7}$	7	$\frac{6}{9}+\frac{1}{9}=\frac{7}{9}$
8	$\frac{4}{4}, \frac{4}{9}$	8	$\frac{8}{9}, \frac{4}{9}$	8	$\frac{9}{12}+\frac{2}{12}=\frac{11}{12}$
9	$\frac{6}{6}, \frac{2}{5}$			9	$\frac{6}{7}+\frac{4}{7}=\frac{10}{7}$
10	$\frac{9}{9}, \frac{1}{3}$			10	$\frac{7}{8}+\frac{1}{8}=\frac{8}{8}$
11	$\frac{2}{2}, \frac{4}{7}$			11	$\frac{3}{9}+\frac{5}{9}=\frac{8}{9}$
12	$\frac{16}{16}, \frac{1}{2}$			12	$\frac{9}{10}+\frac{7}{10}=\frac{16}{10}$

No.	Pg 70 Answer	No.	Pg 71 Answer	No.	Pg 72 Answer
1	$\dfrac{12}{18} - \dfrac{4}{18} = \dfrac{8}{18}$	1	$\dfrac{2}{2}$	1	12
2	$\dfrac{4}{7} - \dfrac{1}{7} = \dfrac{3}{7}$	2	$\dfrac{3}{3}$	2	12
3	$\dfrac{7}{9} - \dfrac{4}{9} = \dfrac{3}{9}$	3	$\dfrac{4}{4}$	3	10
4	$\dfrac{4}{5} - \dfrac{3}{5} = \dfrac{1}{5}$	4	$\dfrac{3}{3}$	4	40
5	$\dfrac{3}{7} - \dfrac{2}{7} = \dfrac{1}{7}$	5	$\dfrac{8}{8}$	5	5
6	$\dfrac{6}{7} - \dfrac{5}{7} = \dfrac{1}{7}$	6	$\dfrac{5}{5}$	6	90
7	$\dfrac{9}{9} - \dfrac{6}{9} = \dfrac{3}{9}$	7	$\dfrac{3}{3}$	7	80
8	$\dfrac{8}{9} - \dfrac{3}{9} = \dfrac{5}{9}$	8	$\dfrac{11}{11}$	8	16
9	$\dfrac{6}{7} - \dfrac{3}{7} = \dfrac{3}{7}$	9	$\dfrac{9}{9}$	9	28
10	$\dfrac{8}{9} - \dfrac{2}{9} = \dfrac{6}{9}$			10	90
11	$\dfrac{5}{6} - \dfrac{2}{6} = \dfrac{3}{6}$			11	14
12	$\dfrac{8}{9} - \dfrac{5}{9} = \dfrac{3}{9}$			12	55
				13	128
				14	15
				15	50
				16	80
				17	12
				18	15
				19	6
				20	16

Pg 73		Pg 74	
No.	Answer	No.	Answer
1	$\dfrac{4}{8} + \dfrac{1}{8} = \dfrac{5}{8}$	1	$\dfrac{10}{20} - \dfrac{6}{20} = \dfrac{4}{20}$
2	$\dfrac{4}{12} + \dfrac{6}{12} = \dfrac{10}{12}$	2	$\dfrac{14}{15} - \dfrac{12}{15} = \dfrac{2}{15}$
3	$\dfrac{6}{21} + \dfrac{5}{21} = \dfrac{11}{21}$	3	$\dfrac{13}{18} - \dfrac{6}{18} = \dfrac{7}{18}$
4	$\dfrac{4}{28} + \dfrac{21}{28} = \dfrac{25}{28}$	4	$\dfrac{35}{40} - \dfrac{20}{40} = \dfrac{15}{40}$
5	$\dfrac{30}{50} + \dfrac{12}{50} = \dfrac{42}{50}$	5	$\dfrac{40}{48} - \dfrac{29}{48} = \dfrac{11}{48}$
6	$\dfrac{6}{24} + \dfrac{15}{24} = \dfrac{21}{24}$	6	$\dfrac{16}{24} - \dfrac{15}{24} = \dfrac{1}{24}$
7	$\dfrac{21}{48} + \dfrac{16}{48} = \dfrac{37}{48}$	7	$\dfrac{36}{49} - \dfrac{21}{49} = \dfrac{15}{49}$
8	$\dfrac{45}{81} + \dfrac{12}{81} = \dfrac{57}{81}$	8	$\dfrac{45}{54} - \dfrac{29}{54} = \dfrac{16}{54}$
9	$\dfrac{9}{36} + \dfrac{18}{36} = \dfrac{27}{36}$	9	$\dfrac{63}{81} - \dfrac{54}{81} = \dfrac{9}{81}$
10	$\dfrac{28}{63} + \dfrac{5}{63} = \dfrac{33}{63}$	10	$\dfrac{54}{63} - \dfrac{35}{63} = \dfrac{19}{63}$
11	$\dfrac{39}{72} + \dfrac{24}{72} = \dfrac{63}{72}$	11	$\dfrac{27}{48} - \dfrac{24}{48} = \dfrac{3}{48}$
12	$\dfrac{17}{56} + \dfrac{35}{56} = \dfrac{52}{56}$	12	$\dfrac{70}{100} - \dfrac{50}{100} = \dfrac{20}{100}$

Pg 75	
No.	**Answer**
1	$5\frac{10}{12}$
2	$6\frac{4}{9}$
3	$7\frac{4}{5}$
4	$2\frac{20}{23}$
5	$13\frac{6}{8}$
6	$13\frac{10}{15}$
7	$13\frac{30}{39}$
8	$12\frac{9}{10}$
9	$4\frac{5}{19}$
10	$3\frac{5}{8}$
11	$3\frac{6}{16}$
12	$5\frac{4}{6}$
13	$5\frac{4}{25}$
14	$11\frac{1}{10}$
15	$8\frac{27}{44}$

	Pg 76		Pg 77
No.	Answer	No.	Answer
1	$5\frac{5}{10} = 5\frac{1}{2}$	1	$\frac{13}{3}$
2	$9\frac{9}{12} = 9\frac{3}{4}$	2	$\frac{38}{4}$
3	$9\frac{6}{18} = 9\frac{1}{3}$	3	$\frac{13}{2}$
4	$8\frac{4}{8} = 8\frac{1}{2}$	4	$\frac{32}{5}$
5	$12\frac{12}{24} = 12\frac{1}{2}$	5	$\frac{95}{10}$
6	$15\frac{18}{36} = 15\frac{1}{2}$	6	$\frac{21}{5}$
7	$11\frac{21}{56} = 11\frac{3}{8}$	7	$\frac{25}{7}$
8	$14\frac{45}{81} = 14\frac{5}{9}$	8	$\frac{14}{3}$
9	$3\frac{8}{16} = 3\frac{1}{2}$	9	$\frac{26}{5}$
10	$12\frac{4}{12} = 12\frac{1}{3}$	10	$\frac{30}{3}$
11	$8\frac{14}{28} = 8\frac{1}{2}$	11	$\frac{27}{5}$
12	$12\frac{6}{9} = 12\frac{2}{3}$	12	$\frac{18}{8}$
13	$39\frac{28}{42} = 39\frac{2}{3}$	13	$\frac{52}{5}$
14	$18\frac{18}{63} = 18\frac{2}{7}$	14	$\frac{27}{3}$
15	$25\frac{12}{21} = 25\frac{4}{7}$	15	$\frac{69}{11}$
16	$11\frac{20}{50} = 11\frac{2}{5}$	16	$\frac{16}{3}$
		17	$\frac{37}{22}$
		18	$\frac{24}{9}$
		19	$\frac{34}{4}$
		20	$\frac{32}{3}$

Pg 78	
No.	Answer
1	7
2	4
3	3
4	9
5	8
6	31
7	5
8	42
9	$2\frac{3}{6}$
10	$2\frac{2}{4}$
11	$3\frac{1}{2}$
12	$2\frac{3}{8}$
13	$5\frac{3}{4}$
14	$8\frac{2}{3}$
15	$5\frac{5}{9}$
16	$5\frac{6}{8}$

Chapter 5 – Decimals

Pg 80		Pg 81		Pg 82		Pg 83	
No.	Answer	No.	Answer	No.	Answer	No.	Answer
1	10.83	1	19.44	1	40.365	1	971.2
2	11.55	2	17.82	2	16.728	2	522.16
3	17.01	3	18.61	3	108.352	3	233.49
4	74.83	4	22.83	4	13.774	4	480.18
5	71.38	5	264.57	5	68.174	5	1,535.15
6	71.22	6	85.62	6	131.437	6	856.17
		7	93.31	7	109.184	7	839.27
		8	115.88	8	116.236	8	829.72
		9	1,000.77	9	77.166	9	1,019.78

Pg 84		Pg 85	
No.	Answer	No.	Answer
1	points: 75.4 rebounds: 16.2	1	165.93
2	18.5	2	130.62
3	19.55	3	337.26
4	40.34	4	443.47
		5	898.79
		6	1,328.24
		7	913.05
		8	1,676.61
		9	98.011
		10	47.257
		11	134.537
		12	110.116
		13	752.03
		14	1,591.924
		15	1,292.80
		16	675.154
		17	1,161.326
		18	1,130.321
		19	1,107.368
		20	1,526.574

Pg 86		Pg 87		Pg 88		Pg 89	
No.	Answer	No.	Answer	No.	Answer	No.	Answer
1	2,292.203	1	8,947.33	1	4.55	1	49.97
2	1,024.508	2	14,437.96	2	13.45	2	27.68
3	2,369.367	3	10,098.36	3	27.4	3	13.89
4	1,589.946	4	9,065.53	4	559.93	4	15.96
5	1,602.404	5	20,055.64	5	88.65	5	1.17
6	2,443.596	6	14,216.45	6	298.91	6	30.6
7	2,241.336	7	12,316.47			7	18.17
8	1,953.052	8	8,814.81			8	46.75
9	1,862.583	9	10,754.98			9	17.56
10	2,328.303	10	13,061.62				
11	1,192.89	11	10,903.89				
12	2,315.809	12	11,889.87				
13	3,293.375	13	23,148.84				
14	2,686.997	14	12,299.29				
15	2,241.406	15	10,762.47				
16	2,921.589	16	23,018.72				

Pg 90		Pg 91		Pg 92		Pg 93	
No.	Answer	No.	Answer	No.	Answer	No.	Answer
1	592.45	1	79.312	1	49.33	1	883.23
2	802.22	2	36.252	2	326.39	2	2,100.45
3	293.5	3	55.411	3	105.26	3	4,459.81
4	37.64	4	60.407	4	123.73	4	2,713.83
5	112.21	5	11.221	5	241.84	5	5,062.25
6	466.93	6	338.301	6	341.48	6	7,294.40
7	499.62	7	16.151	7	347.08	7	5,944.50
8	103.94	8	6.905	8	169.62	8	1,416.89
9	279.49	9	579.732	9	534.35	9	2,339.55
				10	465.36	10	4,778.22
				11	87.14	11	2,424.61
				12	33.44	12	1,172.31
				13	44.791	13	452.891
				14	20.014	14	632.574
				15	13.269	15	626.454
				16	5.9	16	316.231
				17	21.28	17	94.845
				18	36.574	18	202.634
				19	42.545	19	153.408
				20	25.487	20	561.034

Pg 94		Pg 95		Pg 96		Pg 97	
No.	Answer	No.	Answer	No.	Answer	No.	Answer
1	17.3123	1	1.35	1	$152.40	1	$519.58
2	39.8811	2	26.82	2	$328.14	2	$333.97
3	21.4554	3	53.96	3	$387.76	3	$777.29
4	45.6271	4	2.41	4	$227.07	4	$642.55
5	164.069			5	$447.00	5	$928.53
6	168.894			6	$1,433.61	6	$1,528.24
7	20.514			7	$585.61	7	$1,213.41
8	109.208			8	$1,281.75	8	$1,605.84
9	10,213.10			9	$889.47	9	$702.13
10	1,588.44			10	$1,343.92	10	$1,236.92
11	6,203.53			11	$771.90	11	$1,142.83
12	5.35945			12	$1,076.38	12	$978.09
13	2,176.26			13	$1,452.60	13	$2,496.52
14	202.851			14	$1,132.89	14	$2,007.13
15	2.03419			15	$1,109.55	15	$2,701.26
16	12.2159			16	$882.25	16	$2,751.54
17	74,083.40					17	1,364.77
18	20,618.30					18	$1,139.83
19	13,601.50					19	$1,405.49
20	1,078.77					20	$1,875.55

Pg 98		Pg 99		Pg 100		Pg 101	
No.	Answer	No.	Answer	No.	Answer	No.	Answer
1	$2.38	1	$167.57	1	53.12	1	22.737
2	$3.35	2	$235.72	2	9.57	2	5.891
3	$1.85	3	$221.39	3	29.48	3	4.446
4	$2.47	4	$205.16	4	21.24	4	34.368
5	$5.31	5	$335.66	5	13.05	5	19.032
6	$1.79	6	$685.64	6	56.95	6	27.36
7	$3.82	7	$141.12	7	13.23	7	35.336
8	$4.63	8	$65.73	8	60.76	8	1,440.60
9	$2.86	9	$213.18	9	44.66	9	8.2917
10	$2.14	10	$508.08	10	77.9	10	194.88
11	$1.75	11	$62.57	11	65.12	11	.24153
12	$4.22	12	$671.71	12	33.63	12	995.9
13	$59.09	13	$275.12	13	30.38	13	32.074
14	$104.35	14	$488.63	14	10.75	14	293.26
15	$76.62	15	$34.40	15	33.93	15	6.6744
16	$222.33	16	$524.21			16	185.52
17	$451.09	17	$212.65			17	2.058
18	$321.63	18	$175.49			18	223.29
19	$441.51	19	$248.53			19	5,603.40
20	$82.86	20	$216.79			20	4.0736
						21	31.524
						22	395.34
						23	26.978
						24	19.91
						25	442.96

Pg 102		Pg 103	
No.	Answer	No.	Answer
1	124.576	1	938.448
2	14.5497	2	357.7665
3	1,656.86	3	449.709
4	167.678	4	1.831536
5	42.526	5	5696.46
6	14.1327	6	1,242.448
7	340.548	7	318.8694
8	110.451	8	304.3408
9	927.5	9	1,371.806
10	24.2934	10	404.9125
11	7303.12	11	248.5998
12	1,762.18	12	27,895.43
13	360.549	13	86.8795
14	509.819	14	185.8618
15	270.338	15	257.2271
16	262.145	16	54,917.25
17	1,653.75	17	624.9639
18	78.4101	18	6,041.386
19	55.062	19	107.1348
20	192.576	20	41,661.18
21	8,360.52		
22	8,045.73		
23	35.1978		
24	27.6216		
25	745.129		

Chapter 6 – Geometry

Pg 108		Pg 109	
No.	Answer	No.	Answer
1	74 x 74 = 5,476 in.^{2}	1	11in. x 6in. ÷ 2 = 33 in.^{2}
2	134ft. x 749ft. = 100,366 ft.^{2}	2	12ft. x 17ft. ÷ 2 = 102 ft.^{2}
3	205in. x 205in. = 42,025 in.^{2}	3	5in. x 14in. ÷ 2 = 35 in.^{2}
4	299ft. x 436ft. = 130,364 ft.^{2}	4	75in. x 46in. ÷ 2 =1,72 5in.^{2}
5	637in. x 637in. = 405,769 in.^{2}	5	94in. x 89in. ÷ 2 = 4,183 in.^{2}
6	507yd. x 1,262yd. = 639,834 yd.^{2}	6	112ft. x 156ft. ÷ 2 = 8,736 ft.^{2}

Pg 110		Pg 111	
No.	Answer	No.	Answer
1	6 x 6 = 36 ft.^{2}	1	6 + 9 x 6 ÷ 2 = 45 yds.^{2}
2	13 x 5 = 65 in.^{2}	2	24 + 16 x 8 ÷ 2 = 160 ft.^{2}
3	15 x 17 = 255 ft.^{2}	3	20 + 32 x 12 ÷ 2 = 312 in.^{2}
4	75 x 45 = 3,375 ft.^{2}	4	55 + 110 x 40 ÷ 2 = 3,300 ft.^{2}
5	136 x 115 = 15,640 in.^{2}	5	136 + 175 x 212 ÷ 2 = 32,966 in.^{2}
6	563 x 599 = 337,237 ft.^{2}	6	250 + 210 x 88 ÷ 2 = 20,240 in.^{2}

Pg 112		Pg 113	
No.	Answer	No.	Answer
1	55 + 36 + 42 + 67 = 197 yd.	1	12 + 4 + 4 + 6 + 8 + 10 = 44 yd.
2	125 + 89 + 89 + 125 = 428 ft.	2	4 + 13 + 1 + 12 + 15 = 45 ft.
3	123 + 215 + 107 + 324 = 769 in.	3	88 + 200 + 96 + 88 + 105 + 88 + 411 = 1,076 in.
4	75 + 347 + 62 + 289 +101 = 874 ft.	4	8 + 8 + 8 + 8 + 8 + 8 + 8 + 8 = 64 ft.
5	572 + 635 + 468 = 1,675 in.	5	20 + 20 + 5 + 15 + 15 + 5 = 80 in.
6	917 + 234 + 705 + 917 = 2,773 yd.	6	35 + 4 + 17 + 20 + 19 + 15 + 4 = 114 in.
		7	60 + 55 + 34 + 27 + 10 = 186 ft.
		8	7 + 18 + 19 + 7 + 22 + 8 + 23 = 104 in.
		9	100 + 100 + 25 + 25 + 27 + 50 + 25 = 352 yd.

- 39 -

Pg 114	
No.	Answer
1	vertex- 1, ray- 2, point- 3
2	vertex-1, line segment-2, point -5
3	line-1, ray-2, point-2
4	line-1, ray-2, vertex-1, point-2
5	ray-3, vertex-2, point-4
6	ray-1, line segment-1, vertex-1, point-4
7	ray- 3, vertex-2, point-4
8	ray-2, line-2, point-2

Pg 115			
No.	Answer		
1	Angle: ABC	Vertex: B	Rays: AB, CB
2	Angle: 123	Vertex: 2	Rays: 12, 23
3	Angle: QRS	Vertex: R	Rays: SR, QR
4	Angle: XYZ	Vertex: Y	Rays: XY, YZ
5	Angle: 456	Vertex: 5	Rays: 45, 56
6	Angle: EFG	Vertex: F	Rays: EF, EG
7	Angle: MNO	Vertex: N	Rays: MN, NO
8	Angle: 678	Vertex: 7	Rays: 67, 78
9	Angle: DEF	Vertex: E	Rays: FE, DE
10	Angle: 789	Vertex: 8	Rays: 78, 89
11	Angle: 012	Vertex: 1	Rays: 01, 12
12	Angle: UVW	Vertex: V	Rays: UV, VW

Pg 117

1. Pyramid
   a. 4
   b.6
   c. 4

2. Cylinder
   a. 0
   b. 2
   c. 3

3. Cube
   a. 8
   b. 12
   c. 6

Pg 118

1. Cone
   a. 1
   b. 1
   c. 2

2. Cuboid
   a. 8
   b. 12
   c. 6

3. Pyramid
   a. 5
   b. 8
   c. 5

Pg 120

No.	Answer		
1	Circle: A	Radius: AB, AC, AD	Diameter: BC
2	Circle: E	Radius: EF, EH, EG	Diameter: FG
3	Circle: X	Radius: XW, XZ, XY	Diameter: WY
4	Circle: R	Radius: RQ, RS,RT	Diameter: QT
5	Circle: M	Radius: ML, MN, MO	Diameter: LO
6	Circle: X	Radius: XR, XA, XP	Diameter: AR

Pg 121		Pg 122	
No.	Answer	No.	Answer
1	18 ÷ 2 = 9 cm.	1	12 x 2 = 24 in.
2	36 ÷ 2 = 18 in.	2	29 x 2 = 58 cm.
3	112 ÷ 2 = 56 ft.	3	89 x 2 = 178 ft.
4	388 ÷ 2 = 194 in.	4	113 x 2 = 226 cm.
5	956 ÷ 2 = 478 ft.	5	624 x 2 = 1,24 in.
6	3,624 ÷ 2 = 1,812 cm.	6	2,935x 2 = 5,870 ft.

Pg 123

No.	Answer
1	345.4 in.
2	226.08 cm.
3	942 ft.
4	120.89 ft.
5	3,337.192 in.
6	21.64716 cm.

Chapter 7 - Graphs

Pg 126		Pg 127	
No.	Answer	No.	Answer
1	Game 5	1	60
2	Game 1	2	35
3	52 Goals	3	45
4	4 Goals	4	30
5	7 Goals	5	45
6	16 Goals	6	50
7	25 Goals	7	65
8	Games 2 and 8	8	25
		9	40
		10	20
		11	25
		12	5
		13	25
		14	5
		15	20
		16	30
		17	45
		18	10

Pg 128

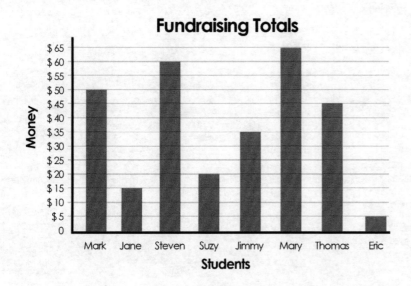

- 43 -

Pg 128	
No.	Answer
1	$45
2	$20
3	$15
4	$35
5	$50
6	$60
7	$65
8	$5
9	$55
10	$15
11	$15
12	$45
13	$45
14	$30

Pg 129	
No.	Answer
1	2012
2	2011
3	85 degrees
4	50 degrees
5	55 degrees
6	Feb
7	July
8	5 degrees
9	90 degrees
10	60 degrees
11	55 degrees
12	10 degrees
13	Stayed the same
14	2011

Pg 130

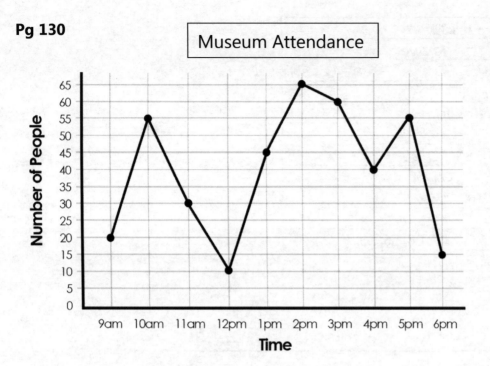

Museum Attendance

Pg 130	
No.	**Answer**
1	2pm
2	12pm
3	10
4	20
5	40
6	25
7	20
8	40
9	12pm - 1pm
10	5pm - 6pm

Pg 131	
No.	Answer
1	A10, C10, C7, E7
2	E10, I10, F7, H7
3	J10, J8, O10, O8
4	Q7, S10, T7
5	A6, A4, B4, B3, D3, D6
6	B2, B1, E5, E2, G5, G1
7	H6, H5, I7, I4, J7, J4, K6, K5
8	I3, I1, L3, O1
9	L7, L4, O5, O4, P7, P6, S6, S5
10	P2, Q4, Q1, S4, S1, T2

Pg 132

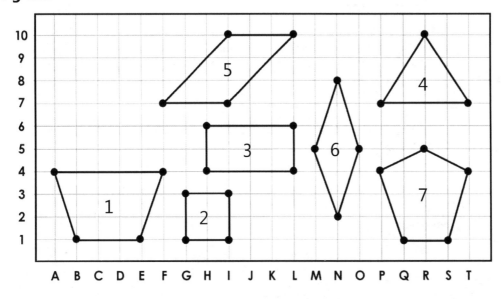

Pg 132	
No.	Answer
1	trapezoid
2	square
3	rectangle
4	triangle
5	parallelogram
6	rhombus
7	pentagon

Pg 133		Pg 135	
No.	Answer	No.	Answer
1	Art	1	Tennis shoes
2	Math	2	Tennis shoes
3	Science	3	Tennis shoes
4	Reading	4	Boots
5	Puppies	5	Sandals
6	Fish	6	Tennis shoes
7	Kittens	7	Boots
8	Gerbil	8	Boots
		9	Boots
		10	Sandals

Pg 136

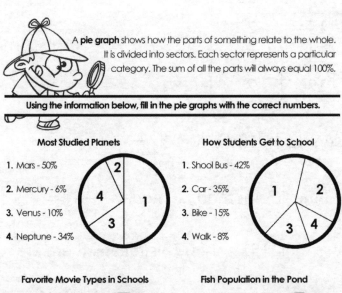

A **pie graph** shows how the parts of something relate to the whole. It is divided into sectors. Each sector represents a particular category. The sum of all the parts will always equal 100%.

Using the information below, fill in the pie graphs with the correct numbers.

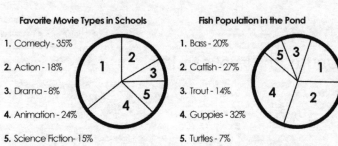

Most Studied Planets

1. Mars - 50%
2. Mercury - 6%
3. Venus - 10%
4. Neptune - 34%

How Students Get to School

1. Shool Bus - 42%
2. Car - 35%
3. Bike - 15%
4. Walk - 8%

Favorite Movie Types in Schools

1. Comedy - 35%
2. Action - 18%
3. Drama - 8%
4. Animation - 24%
5. Science Fiction- 15%

Fish Population in the Pond

1. Bass - 20%
2. Catfish - 27%
3. Trout - 14%
4. Guppies - 32%
5. Turtles - 7%

Practice Test Answers

Practice Test #1

Answers and Explanations

1. A: The digit 5 is in the 5th column, which is the ten thousands column. Therefore the digit represents the value 50,000.

2. C: Robinson has the highest number of points. The number of goals and assists need to be added to determine this.

Player	Goals	Assists	Points
Phillips	2	23	25
Jackson	5	17	22
Robinson	13	15	28
Miller	8	19	27

3. B: $\frac{15}{4}$. The value of 3 is equivalent to $\frac{12}{4}$. Therefore, $3\frac{3}{4} = \frac{12}{4} + \frac{3}{4} = \frac{15}{4}$. Another way of
of finding this is sometimes called the "C" method. $3\frac{3}{4}$ equals $\frac{4\times3+3}{4} = \frac{15}{4}$.

4. C: The largest multiple of 12 less than 151 is 144. This means there are $151 - 144 = 7$ eggs left over.

5. C: Count from the 3: tenths, hundredths, thousandths.

6. D: A diagram of the plot would look like this:

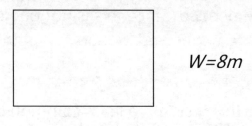

$W=8m$

$L=3W=24\ m$

The perimeter of a rectangle is the formula $P = 2L + 2W$ which produces $2(24) + 2(8) = 48 + 16 = 64\ m$.

7. Part A: B: The pattern in the table is that the number of customers is increasing by 25 each week. This means that there should be $205 + 25 = 230$ customers expected in week 4.

Week	Customers
1	155
2	180
3	205
4	230

+25
+25
+25

Part B: $2760: From Part A you know there will be 230 people in week 4. If each meal is $12 then just multiply to get the answer. $230 \times 12 = 2760$

8. 3: The area of a rectangular prism is $A = L \times W \times H$. The problem gives L, W, and A. To get H just divide A by L and W. $144 \div 8 = 18 \div 6 = 3$. So $H=3$.

9. A: This is a simple subtraction problem with decimals. Line up the decimals and subtract 9 from 8. Since this can't be done, borrow 10 from the 5. Cross out the 5 and make it 4. Now subtract 9 from 18 to get 9. Subtract 3 from 4 and get 1. Place the decimal point before the 1.

10. D: The recipe is being multiplied by 4 in this problem, therefore $\frac{1}{8} = \frac{4}{32}$ so a total of 4 cups of milk are needed. Since this is not one of the choices, a conversion is needed. 1 pint = 2 cups and 1 quart = 2 pints, therefore 1 quart = 4 cups.

11. A: To solve a problem like this first find a least common denominator. For 2, 4, and 5 that would be 20. Then convert each fraction to twentieths. $\frac{2}{5} = \frac{8}{20}, \frac{3}{4} = \frac{15}{20}, and \frac{1}{2} = \frac{10}{20}$. Next perform the operations that were given. $\frac{8}{20} + \frac{15}{20} - \frac{10}{20} = \frac{13}{20}$.

12. A: To solve, test each answer. Notice that in (A), the numerator has been multiplied by 3 to get 12. The denominator has been multiplied by 3 to get 21. In (B) the numerator has been multiplied by 4 and the denominator has been multiplied by 5. In (C), the numerator has been multiplied by 3 and the denominator has been multiplied by 4. In (D), the numerator has been multiplied by 4 and the denominator has been multiplied by a number less than 4.

13. 10.92: $A = L \times W$, so multiplying $4.2 \times 2.6 = 10.92$. The area of the card is 10.92 sq inches.

14. B: The total number of Evercell batteries is $(4 \times E)$ and the total number of Durapower batteries is $(6 \times D)$. The sum of the two is the total number of batteries in the store.

15. 3.08: To find the total distance multiply the number of laps times the distance of one lap. $11 \times .28 = 3.08$

16. .375, .71, .85: $.3 \times 1.25 = .375$

$1.22 - .85 + .34 = .37 + .34 = .71$

$(.22 + 1.48) \times .5 = (1.7) \times .5 = .85$

17. B: One property of parallelograms is that the opposite sides are parallel. This means $\overline{QS} \parallel \overline{RT}$.

18. A: The rectangular prism volume formula $V = l \times w \times h$ is used here. $210 = 7 \times 5 \times h$. Dividing both sides by 35 gives the answer $h = 6$ inches.

19. Divide the number of yards by 1760, the number of yards in 1 mile. $\frac{18335}{1760} \approx \mathbf{10.42}$ **miles.**

20. B: There are 36 out of 100 yellow cars in the sample. Since the parking lot has $\frac{1}{4}$ as many cars as the sample, $\frac{1}{4}$ as many yellow cars should be expected.

21. A: $C = \frac{3}{4}(100) + 20$. Since $\frac{1}{4}$ of the original $100 was sent to the savings account, $\frac{3}{4}$ of the money was kept in cash. The bonus was then added afterward.

22. C: Use approximation to solve this problem quickly: $25 \times \$3 = \$75$. The actual cost to fill the tank was $25.2 \times \$2.98 = \$75.10$.

23. D: The order of operations is parentheses, exponents, multiply, divide, add, subtract. So for this problem it would be: $8 \times (5 - 2) + (4 + 5) = 8 \times 3 + 9 = 24 + 9 = 33$

24. C: Add the 1 hour and 30 minutes to find that Janice finishes her homework at 4:15 PM. Next, add 1 hour and 45 minutes to find that Janice returns home at 6:00 PM.

25. A: The simplest way to compare the two pieces of pie is to find a common dominator for both fractions. The older daughter was given 2/5 of the pie, while the younger daughter was given 1/3 of the pie. The least common dominator for the two fractions is 15. Therefore, the older daughter received 6/15 of the pie and the younger daughter received 5/15 of the pie. 6/15 is larger than 5/15; therefore, the older daughter received a larger slice of the pie.

26. 4.43: When a problem asks for the difference use subtraction. $14.67 - 10.24 = 4.43$.

27. A: Translate the point 5 units to the right and 4 units down to find the location of the lighthouse.

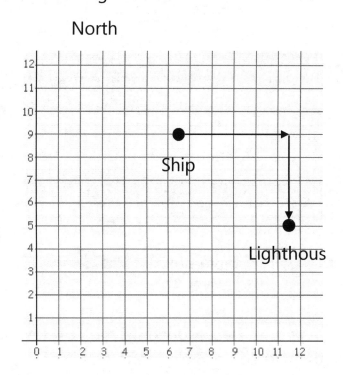

28. D: Plotting the values on a number line demonstrates that this is the only value not in the normal range.

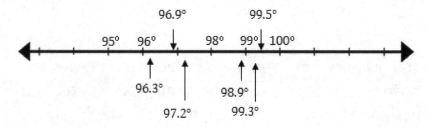

29. B: Use the formula for finding the mean: $\frac{sum\ of\ values}{number\ of\ values}$.
$$\frac{9+16+13+20+22}{5} = \frac{80}{5} = 16.$$

30.

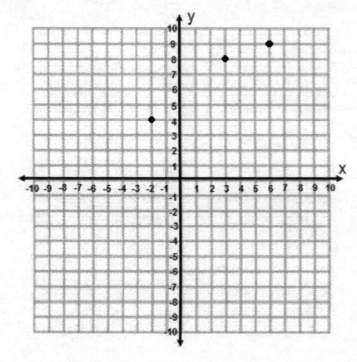

31. B: Divide 92 by 14. $92 \div 14 = 6\,R\,8$. Since 8 is not enough for another team, a total of 6 teams can be formed.

32. Part A: B: By the definition of an isosceles trapezoid, the legs (non-parallel sides) are congruent.

Part B: A: Since the figure is defined as an isosceles, it is known that $\overline{PS}$ and $\overline{QR}$ are parallel and not congruent in length.

33. C:
Expressing $\frac{31}{8} = 3\frac{7}{8}$ makes this easier to see.

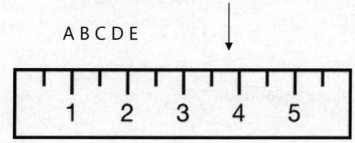

34. C: The points are marked on the figure below.

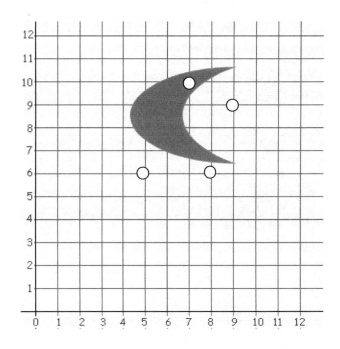

35. C: $1\frac{7}{10}$ is read as one and seven tenths. The 1 can be converted to an equivalent fraction of

$\frac{10}{10}$ and is shown as all ten parts of the first ten section are shaded. $\frac{7}{10}$ indicates that only seven of the ten parts are shaded in the second set of ten. Since the 7 is over the denominator of a ten and read as seven tenths, the seven should be placed in the tenths location when in decimal form. This is the first location to the right of the decimal. The correct decimal form for this is 1.7.

36. $26,150: The total amount they made from T.V.'s is $525 \times 36 = $18,900. The total that they make from game systems is $250 \times 29 = $7,250. $18,900 + $7,250 = $26,150

37. B: Since the probability of being born in the spring or summer is being calculated, the probabilities are added. $\frac{7}{20} + \frac{3}{20} = \frac{10}{20} = \frac{1}{2}$.

38. D: Multiplying the number of weeks by 7 and then adding 5 more days gives the desired result. $7 \times 9 + 5 = 68$.

39. D: To find the difference, subtract. It is important to align decimal places. Note, when subtracting here, the digit in the hundredths place in 0.33 has no digit aligned above it. We must add a zero to 1.5 so that we can align the hundredths places correctly. Now we can subtract 33 hundredths from the 50 hundredths to get 17 hundredths. So, we get 1.17 as our correct answer.

40. B: There are 2 green sections on the spinner and the spinner has 6 sections in all. The probability of spinning green is 2 out of 6, when expressed as a fraction is $\frac{2}{6}$. Written in simplest terms, the fraction is $\frac{1}{3}$.

Practice Test #2

Answers and Explanations

1. D: Fifty-seven thousand is 57,000; adding the three hundred forty to that amount gives the correct answer: 57,340.

2. D: Construct a 3rd column representing improvement. This would be the second score minus the first score for each of the students. David has the greatest improvement of 20 words per minute between the two tests.

Student	First score (words per minute)	Second score (words per minute)	Improvement Second – First scores
Alexander	22	39	17
Betty	39	48	9
Carolyn	27	43	16
David	22	42	20

3. C: The value of 7 is equivalent to $\frac{56}{8}$. Therefore, $7\frac{5}{8} = \frac{56}{8} + \frac{5}{8} = \frac{61}{8}$. Another way of finding this is sometimes called the "C" method: $7\frac{5}{8}$ equals $\frac{8 \times 7 + 5}{8} = \frac{61}{8}$.

4. B: The largest multiple of 12 less than 141 is $12 \times 11 = 132$. This leaves $141 - 132 = 9$ donuts remaining.

5. C: Count from the 5: tenths, hundredths, thousandths.

6. 528: First find Donny's weight in pounds. So, 56-23=33, then it can be converted to ounces by multiplying times 16. $33 \times 16 = 528$.

7. A: Use the area formula for a square: $A = s^2$. Solve the equation: $81 = s^2$, $s = \pm 9$. Since the side of the garden is a length, it must be positive, $s = 9$ feet.

8. B: To solve, test each answer. Notice that in (A), the numerator has been multiplied by 9 to get 18. The denominator has been multiplied by 8. These are not equal fractions. In (C) the numerator has been multiplied by 4 and the denominator has been multiplied by 2. These are not equal fractions. In (D) the numerator has been multiplied by 3 and the denominator has been multiplied by 2. These are not equal fractions. In (B), both numerator and denominator have been multiplied by 4.

9. The hundredths place is the second number after the decimal point. When rounding 1-4 rounds down and 5-9 rounds up.

$3.116 \approx 3.12$

$3.081 \approx 3.08$

$3.006 \approx 3.01$

$3.107 \approx 3.11$

10. D: A trapezoid is a quadrilateral with only one pair of opposite sides parallel.
The other three figures in the problem are a rectangle, a rhombus, and a parallelogram (in that order).

11. B: The proportion given is that 1 gallon of cooking oil will make enough popcorn for 256 people, or 128 ounces serves 256 people. Notice that the amount of oil in ounces needed is exactly one half the number of people being served. This means 48 ounces are needed to serve 96 people. The equivalent amount listed in the choices is 3 pints.

12. B: Working the problem backwards, Jody had $29 before she went to the movies. This was half of the money she made at the bake sale. This means 2 × $29 = $58 was made at the bake sale.

13. A: Since all the answers have a 7 as the whole number, multiply 7 x 14. The answer is 98. The remainder is 1.

14. D: Since the marbles are being equally distributed in 4 equal parts, each friend is simply receiving $\frac{1}{4}$ of the marbles.

15. Part A: 1248: To find the total number of rolls multiply the number of rolls in a package times the number of packages, then times the number of boxes. $8 \times 6 \times 26 = 1248$

Part B: 5: To find out how many shipments they need divide 6100 by 1248. $6100 \div 1248 \approx 4.89$. So they would need at least 5 shipments a month.

16. Part A: $\frac{5}{24}$: First you need like denominators. For 6 and 8 that would be 24. $\frac{5}{8} = \frac{15}{24}$ and $\frac{5}{6} = \frac{20}{24}$. So, the second one is $\frac{5}{24}$ bigger.

Part B: $2\frac{1}{24}$: To find the total you will also need to first find like denominators. In this case 24 will also work. So, $\frac{7}{12} = \frac{14}{24}$, then $\frac{15}{24} + \frac{20}{24} + \frac{14}{24} = \frac{49}{24} = 2\frac{1}{24}$

17. B: By definition, the opposite sides of a parallelogram are equal and congruent.

18. D: Use the volume of a rectangular prism formula $V = L \times W \times H$ to determine the length of the tank.

$$200 = L \times 8 \times 5 \rightarrow 200 = 40L \rightarrow L = 5 \text{ feet.}$$

19. C: Dividing the height of Mt. McKinley by the number of feet in a mile gives the correct result. $\frac{20320}{5280} = 3.85$ miles. This rounds to the approximation of 4 miles high.

20. Using the ratio 8 : 20 and noticing that the school has 12 times more students than the classroom. Multiplying the ratio by 12 gives: **96 : 240**.

21. D: The other choices define A. Raising the wholesale price by $1.75. B. Multiplying the wholesale price by 0.25 and then adding $1.50. C. Multiplying the wholesale price by 1.75.

22. B: Since Laura was leaving the movies at 8:15, go backward 2:45 to get the start time of the movie. 2 hours prior was 6:15, and the additional 45 minutes moves the start time back to 5:30 PM.

23. 48: Order of operations are parentheses, exponents, multiplication, division, addition, and subtraction. The steps to solve this problem are:
$3 + (9 - 4) \times (4 + 5) =?$
$3 + 5 \times 9 =?$
$3 + 45 = 48$

24. B: If you add all of the minutes together you get 202. When converted to hours and minutes that is three hours and 22 minutes.

25. B: Unless the rectangular prism is a cube, some of the sides will have different areas than others. Opposite sides will be equal in area.

26. B: $1\frac{5}{10}$ is read as one and five tenths. The 1 can be converted to an equivalent fraction of

$\frac{10}{10}$ and is shown as all ten parts of the first ten section are shaded. $\frac{5}{10}$ indicates that only
five of the ten parts are shaded in the second set of ten. Since the 5 is over the denominator of a ten and read as five tenths, the five should be placed

in the tenths location when in decimal form. This is the first location to the right of the decimal. The correct decimal form for this is 1.5.

27. B: On the plane provided, north is up and west is to the left. Shift point (8, 5) up 2 and left 4 units to obtain the position of the fire.

North

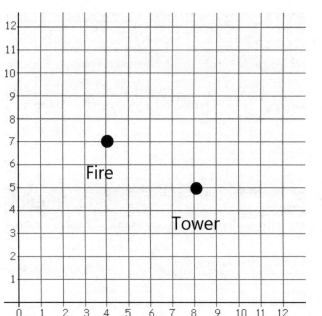

East

28. D: A box that is 13 × 4 × 8 would be 416 cubic inches.

29. C: Use the formula for finding the mean, $mean = \dfrac{sum\ of\ values}{number\ of\ values}$.

$$\frac{22+28+38+48+45}{5} = \frac{180}{5} = 36$$

30. D: If Ice Chest A can hold twice as many drinks as B then that means it can hold 48 drinks. If the larger compartment holds 34 and 48-34=14, then the smaller one holds 14.

31. C: If the average weight of a horse is 1100 lbs, the weight of the horses in the race would be 8 × 1100 = 8800 lbs. Dividing this number by 2000 gives the total weight in tons. $8800\ lbs \times \dfrac{1\ ton}{2000\ lbs} = \dfrac{8800}{2000}\ tons = 4.4\ tons$.

32. The solution is found by finding the whole number part of the quotient when dividing 417 by 18: $417 \div 18 = \mathbf{23\ R\ 3}$. Therefore 23 full boxes can be made and 3 pears would be left over.

33. D: A regular pentagon is a 5 sided figure with all sides equal in length. Therefore the perimeter is $5 \times 6.5 = 32.5$ centimeters.

34. C: Convert $\frac{35}{8}$ to a mixed number using division: $\frac{35}{8} = 4\frac{3}{8}$. Point D is located at $4\frac{1}{2}$ inches, so the length is before D. C is 3 inches, so obviously the length is more than C.

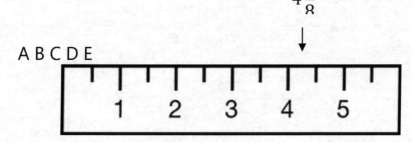

35. B: The four choices are marked on the diagram below.

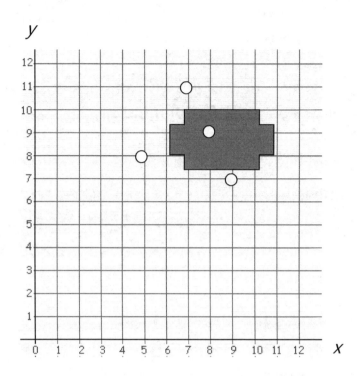

36. C: Since the probability of being either a carpenter or an electrician is being calculated, the probabilities are added. $\frac{13}{50} + \frac{7}{50} = \frac{20}{50} = \frac{2}{5}$.

37. B: This is the only line graph that correctly shows the increase in customers up to 6:00 pm and then the decrease in customers at 8:00 pm.

38. D: To correctly order the numbers in this question, making the decimals all have the same number of digits by adding as many zeros as necessary to the numbers with fewer digits makes them easier to compare. Here, only 17.4 has fewer digits than the others, so add one zero to make it 17.40 (this does not change the value). Now, by comparing place values from left to right of 17.03, 17.4, 17.31, and 17.09, we see that 17.03 is the shortest, 17.09 is the next longest, 17.31 is the third longest, and 17.4 is the longest. Notice the question asked for shortest to longest, not longest to shortest.

39. A: Write 512 then add the decimal in the thousandths place, the third place from the right.

40. C: Divide the numerator and denominator by 14.

Additional Bonus Material

Due to our efforts to try to keep this book to a manageable length, we've created a link that will give you access to all of your additional bonus material.

Please visit http://www.mometrix.com/bonus948/pssag5math to access the information.